Teaching Musical Theatre

The Essential Handbook

16 Ready-to-Go Lesson Plans to Build a Better Actor

A Beat by Beat Book
www.bbbpress.com

Published by Beat by Beat Press. www.bbbpress.com

Table of Contents

All lesson plans are designed as 60-minute sessions for kids age 7-14.
The lessons do not need to be followed in order.

Introduction

The goal of this book is to provide you with specific tools and lesson plans to help you develop the growth of the actors in your musical theatre program.

It can be easy to get lost in the fun and games of musical theatre because, let's face it, musicals are super fun! But it's important to make sure that when teaching musical theatre, every activity is working towards building a foundation that will help your actors be successful onstage. It's incredible what young performers can accomplish when they are given the right goals and guidance.

Similar to *Teaching Drama: The Essential Handbook,* the layout of this resource is meant to recreate the experience of being "in the classroom" observing an expert teacher introduce these concepts to a beginning class of students. Text written in *italics* represents how I would specifically communicate ideas and instructions. You can implement these lessons just as they're written, or use them as a guide and combine them with your own activities.

The first 11 lessons are focused on exploring and discovering the skills necessary to be a great musical theatre actor (singing, dancing, acting). The last 5 lessons are focused on helping students integrate those skills into a fun and effective performance.

These lessons can be used in parallel with specific songs and scenes you are rehearsing (for a musical or cabaret), or they can be used as the backbone of a general musical theatre class. There are suggestions throughout this book for specific songs you can use, but you should free free to replace them with any songs that best match your students' ability and interest.

I hope you enjoy what I think are the best activities for introducing your students to the world of musical theatre!

About the Author

For nearly a decade **DENVER CASADO** has worked as an arts educator with New York City's leading theatre organizations including *Disney Theatricals, New York City Center* and *Young Audiences New York.* Denver's innovative approach to exploring theatre with kids has earned him invitations to speak at the national conferences of the *American Association of Community Theatre* and the *American Alliance for Theatre Education.* In 2011 he was honored with the All Stars Projects' Phyllis Hyman award, in recognition of his important contribution to the creative growth and development of over 20,000 young people in the NYC public school system. Denver is a graduate of New York University's Steinhardt School of Education.

Lesson Activity Overview

Lesson 1
Music Cross
What is a Musical?
Musical Theatre Beginnings
Musical Theatre Then & Now

Lesson 2
Confidence & Relaxation
Vocal Warm Up
Emotional Staircase
Newsies Exploration
Emotional Staircase Improv

Lesson 3
Send the Clap
Vocal Warm-Up
Musical Colors
Music Match
Story Soundtrack

Lesson 4
Send the Clap, Part 2
Vocal Warm-Up
Slow Motion Pantomime
"My Treehouse" Song Transition

Lesson 5
Sound Ball
How the Voice Works
Stage 1: Breathing
Balloon Demonstration
Vocal Roller Coaster
"My Treehouse"

Lesson 6
Say Your Name
Articulation
Vocal Warm-Ups
Singing Vowels
"My Treehouse"

Lesson 7
Practice with 8-counts
Dance & Movement in Musicals
Choreography Formations
Choreography Steps
Choreograph a Song

Lesson 8
Copycat Dance
Vocal Warm-Up
Movement Exploration
Student-Led Choreography

Lesson 9
Vocal Warm-Up
Cold Read
Acting a Song
"My Treehouse" Review
Personalize the Song
Perform "My Treehouse"

Lesson 10
10 Dollars, Please
Vocal Warm-Up
Who Are You Singing To?
Sing with the Eyes
Perform "My Treehouse"

Lesson 11
Join the World
The Role of the Ensemble
World of Newsies
World of Anything

Lesson 12
Circle Perfection
Create Performance Rubric
Vocal Warm-Up
Introduce Solo Songs
Introduce Ensemble Songs

Lesson 13
Epic Story Mode
Vocal Warm-Up
Rehearse Ensemble Numbers
Review Solo Songs
Perform Song as Monologue
Solo Performance Practice

Lesson 14
Imagine Your Character…
Vocal Warm-Up
Rehearse Ensemble Numbers
Optional Rehearsal Activities
Performance Order Sign-Up

Lesson 15
Shake it Out
Vocal Warm-Up
Performance

Lesson 16
Group Massage
Video Recording Assessment
Final Reflection

Lesson 1: Discovering Musical Theatre

OBJECTIVE: Students will discover how musical theatre is an exciting, contemporary art form that involves telling stories through a seamless integration of dialogue, song and dance.

MATERIALS:

- Music player/contrasting musical theatre song clips (instrumental preferred)
- Large writing surface (dry-erase board, chart paper, etc.)
- 5 Show Cards (Index cards with information about a specific musical (see **Pages 6-7**)

WARM UP: Music Cross

- Tell the students that you are a Broadway director looking to cast the next big Broadway musical! They must listen closely and perform the following task with full enthusiasm.
- For this "audition", students must gather on one side of the "stage" (from this point on *stage* will refer to any large playing area).
- Play the contrasting musical theatre song clips. You can jump from track to track as desired.
- When you begin playing music, students must cross the stage two at a time "acting out" the music as best as possible. They should put the music in their bodies, their faces, their shoulders, their eyes.
- Every so often, ask the students to pause and share how they feel. If the students are adventurous, consider asking them to *sing* how they feel.
- After everyone has gone as pairs, have the entire class move around the stage letting loose, acting out the music to the best of their ability.
- After a minute, stop the music, ask the class to take a deep breath in, a deep breath out, then form a sitting circle in 3…2…1.
- Ask the class: *Why do you think we started with this activity as we begin to learn about musical theatre?*

> When giving instructions it's best to be as clear and concise as possible, ideally with a "3…2…1…" countdown (when appropriate). This will encourage the students to stay focused even during transitions.

GREETING:

- Briefly introduce yourself and your experience as an actor/performer. Add a fun personal tidbit (about why you love musicals, or your first experience seeing a Broadway show, etc.)
- Then one-by-one, go around the circle and have each student share their name, their favorite musical, and why they like it.
- Explain that over the next few weeks we'll be training for Broadway. We'll be learning all about musical theatre and how to become Broadway-quality actors, singers and dancers!

EXPLORATION: What is a Musical?

- Have the class take a seat facing the writing surface.
- Ask the class the following questions and allow them to share their answers:
  - *What is a musical?*
  - *How is a musical different than a concert?* (A concert doesn't have a story.)
  - *Why would you have singing be part of telling a story? In real life we don't spontaneously burst into song.* (You can act out a funny example of this.)
- Eventually students will say the words "feeling" or "emotion".
- *Music has this incredible way of making us feel something, without any words at all. And when you add words to that feeling and put it inside of a story, you can feel what the characters are going through much more strongly than without music. And that makes the story much more exciting and entertaining. In musicals, characters sing when they are at a point of high emotion.*
- Write the following quote up on the board:

> *Words make you think thoughts.*
> *Music makes you feel a feeling.*
> *But a song makes you feel a thought.*
> - E.Y. "Yip" Harburg
> (lyricist of Over the Rainbow)

- Ask the students to name some of their favorite songs from musicals (live musicals or animated).
- Make a list on the board. Then next to each song write the character who sings it and what the character is feeling.
- Explain: *When composers, lyricists and playwrights create musicals, they think very hard about every note and every word to tell the most entertaining and authentic story.*
- *It is our job as musical theatre actors to convey the story the best we can through singing, acting and dancing.*
- **That is going to be our focus for this semester.**

ACTIVITY: Musical Theatre Beginnings

- *To become great musical actors, we first need to understand how musicals came to be.*
- Ask the class, *Who would like to come up to the stage and sing a short part of a song you know?* Tell the volunteer to introduce himself, perform the short song section, then encourage the audience to applaud.
- Then ask for another volunteer to come up to show some dance moves. (Introduce him/herself, perform, then applause.)
- Finally, ask for a volunteer to come up to tell a joke or do a trick (i.e. a cartwheel, somersault, etc.)

> Students may vary widely in their knowledge of musical theatre. Some may have participated in school and community shows, while to others it is brand new. Make sure you create an environment where all levels feel comfortable participating in the discussion.

4

- Ask for applause for all three volunteers.
- Explain to the class that what they just saw was a *Vaudeville* show. There was no story - just loosely connected performances - sort of like Saturday Night Live of today. These were the only types of shows that existed before musicals.
- Draw a large horizontal timeline on the board, at the left end write *Vaudeville*, then at the right end write the current year (2017).
- *Musicals are different from Vaudeville. Musicals are the seamless integration of dialogue, song and dance motivated by the demands of plot and character. Surprisingly this is actually a very new thing when compared to other art forms! It wasn't until 1927, less than 100 years ago, that the very first musical as we know them today opened on Broadway. The musical was called Showboat. Written by Jerome Kern and Oscar Hammerstein, it tackled a complicated story with heavy themes where music and lyrics helped to amplify the emotions of the characters and move the plot forward.*
- Draw a dot on the timeline with "1927: Showboat". On the far end draw a dot with "2015: Hamilton".

ACTIVITY: Musical Theatre Then & Now

- *To get a better understanding of how we got from Showboat to Hamilton, I'm going to need your help!*
- Divide the class into 5 groups.
- Give each group a "show card". (see **Page 6-7**)
- Explain that each card contains a musical, the year it opened on Broadway, a short synopsis, and why it was important.
- Give each group 5 minutes to figure out a way to present this information to the class in an exciting way. Every member must be involved.
- Have each group present, then attach the cards up to the timeline in the correct order.
- If time permits, consider playing a short audio clip from each show.

> In addition to learning about musical theatre history, this activity will also help students get to know each other and start to feel comfortable working together.

REFLECTION:

- *Who can describe musical theatre in one sentence?*
- *How is it different from other art forms?*
- *Why do you think musicals are so popular?*
- *Which part of musical theatre - acting, singing, or dancing - do you think you'll enjoy the most?*
- *Drama Journal*: Research one musical not discussed today and create your own "show card" in your journal.*

> * Before your classes begin, instruct every student to bring an empty notebook that will become their "drama journal". (Or provide one for them.) These will be used after every class to explore the lessons further. Encourage the students to use these notebooks however they feel inspired as your semester progresses.

Show Cards for Lesson 1

Oklahoma!
Music by Richard Rodgers
Lyrics by Oscar Hammerstein

Broadway Opening:
1943

Synopsis: Tells the story of cowboys and farmers finding love in rural Oklahoma.

Why does it matter?

- Took the change begun by *Showboat* to the next level
- Became the first true "book musical": where the songs and dances are fully integrated into a rich story that evokes genuine emotion other than laughter

- Was the first huge Broadway hit: Ran for 2,212 performances (the previous longest show ran for less than 500 performances)
- Songs became very popular on the radio (and are still performed as jazz "standards" today)
- Includes a 15-minute "dream ballet"

West Side Story
Music by Leonard Bernstein
Lyrics by Stephen Sondheim
Book by Arthur Laurents

Broadway Opening:
1957

Synopsis: Inspired by Romeo & Juliet, explores the rivalry between the Jets and the Sharks, two teenage street gangs in New York City.

Why does it matter?

- The first musical to take the storytelling elements that *Oklahoma* made popular (a "book musical" with serious subject matter) and added to it a present-day, gritty, urban setting.

- Featured "fighting" through dance and music.
- Used dance as a central part of the storytelling.
- Turned into a film in 1961 - received 10 Oscars and gained huge popularity

Cabaret
Music by John Kander
Lyrics by Fred Ebb

Broadway Opening:
1966

Synopsis: Set in 1931 Berlin, it takes place in a nightclub and revolves around a young American writer and his relationship with 32-year-old cabaret performer.

Why does it matter?

- Introduced a completely different style of storytelling that was less traditional. Unlike a "book musical", the story and songs revolved around a central "idea" instead of a linear plot
- This style of musical is called a "concept musical"

- Whole show takes place inside the nightclub, with performances weaving in and out of story
- The most provocative and challenging musical of its day
- Other "concept musicals" that followed include: Chicago, Company, A Chorus Line, Pippin, Cats, Avenue Q.

Phantom of the Opera

Music by Andrew Lloyd Webber
Lyrics by Charles Hart and Richard Stilgoe.

Broadway Opening:
1988

Synopsis: A lush, romantic story of a an opera singer who becomes obsessed with a mysterious, disfigured musical genius living in the basement of the opera house.

Why does it matter?

- The longest running show on Broadway with over 12,000 performances
- Opened first in London, then on Broadway where it has been playing ever since
- By 2011, it was seen by over 130 million people in 145 cities across 27 countries

- In the 1980's and 90's there was a large group of British "mega-musicals" that dominated Broadway: *Evita, Cats, Les Miserables, Miss Saigon*

Rent

Book, Music & Lyrics by Jonathan Larson

Broadway Opening:
1996

Synopsis: It tells the story of a group of impoverished young artists struggling to survive and create a life in New York City's East Village.

Why does it matter?

- Created a whole new generation of theater fans among young people drawn to the modern story and music
- Mostly sung-through with a gritty, energetic rock score

- Featured non-traditional actors with backgrounds in rock music instead of musical theatre
- Influenced many upcoming musical theatre writers, including Lin-Manuel Miranda (composer of Hamilton)

[   ]
Music by
Lyrics by

Broadway Opening:
[   ]

Synopsis:

Why does it matter?

Lesson 2: Storytelling in Musicals

OBJECTIVE: Students will learn about the "emotional staircase" and how it's the basis of storytelling in musical theatre.

MATERIALS:
- Handheld Mirror
- Newsies YouTube Clip (https://youtu.be/GmKUI_RzfR8)
    - Clip Title: *Newsies - Tony Awards 2012*
- Large writing surface

GREETING:
- Ask the class to recall what 3 things are used to tell stories in musicals (dialogue, song, dance).
- Ask a few students to share their drama journal "Show Card" assignments from the last class.
- *Does anyone know what we call someone who can sing, act and dance? A triple threat.*
- *Our goal is for everyone in this class to become a triple-threat. That's why as we continue to explore and learn about musical theatre, we'll begin every class with a movement and voice warm-up.*

MOVEMENT WARM-UP: Confidence & Relaxation
- Gather the class into a standing circle.
- Take out a pocket mirror.
- Tell the class you will be passing around the mirror. When they receive it, they must strike a strong pose, look into the mirror, say 2 factual things they notice about themselves, and end with "…and that is good!". The whole class will then repeat "That is good!".
- Give a demonstration: (looking into the mirror) *I have short brown hair, and green eyes… and that is good!* Class repeats: *That is good!*
- Pass the mirror around the circle.
- Tell the class you will give them 1-minute to turn to their neighbors and say 2 things they like about him/her…go! *(i.e. I like your shoes, I like that you're funny, etc.)*
- *To be great musical actors, we must be confident in ourselves. We must not worry what other people think because we will often be doing things that seem silly! Musical theatre is an exaggerated art form, so we must feel strong and safe and always be willing to take big risks.*
- Lead the class through a series of stretching/relaxation exercises:
    - *Quietly take a strong breath in, and then slowly let it out in 5 seconds. Repeat 2x.*
    - *Stretch your hands way up to the sky, as far as you can reach. Drop your hands down and touch your toes.*

8

- *Stand up straight, drop your head and roll it around in a circle. Switch directions.*
- *Roll your shoulders back. Roll your shoulders forward.*
- *Take a big breath in. Now let it out shaking out your whole body while buzzing your lips.* Ask the class how they feel. *Great!*

Consider playing calming instrumental music during this exercise.

VOCAL WARM-UP:
- Tell the class to take a seat. *We're now going to warm-up our voices.*
- Explain proper singing position: Sitting at the edge of the seat, with their back up straight. Have everyone give it a try. Walk around positively evaluating their posture. Tell them from now on whenever you call out *"Ready to Sing!"* this is the position they should take.
- Make a quick game out of this: Tell the class to sit like they are lazy on the couch at home watching TV. Then say *Ready to Sing!* and watch as they pop up into position. Repeat a few times between *"lazy on the couch"* and *"Ready to Sing!"*
- Compliment them on how professional they look!
- Instruct the class: *When I say "go", using the sound "Ahh", I want you to sing from your highest note all the way down to your lowest note in 10 seconds. Ready...go!* Do it with them, counting down with your fingers 10 to 1.
- You can joke they sort of sound like a robot powering down =)
- Tell them we're going to do it again, but this time in 5 seconds.
- Then 3 seconds.
- Have the students place their hands on their stomachs and shout "Ha!".
- Explain that this is where the "good air" for singing comes from. They should feel their bellies bounce.
- Introduce Vocal Warm-Up #1 below, an arpeggio on the word "Ha!"

Throughout this book I will be introducing and repeating a variety of vocal warm-ups. Feel free to mix and match as desired based on the age-level of your students and what they respond to. And of course you can add your own as well! You can see all the vocal warm-ups on Pages 58-59 in the bonus section.

We will go more in depth with proper singing technique in Lessons 5 & 6.

Keep repeating a half-step higher, 4 or 5 more times.

- *Now our bodies and voices are warmed up and we're ready to learn.*

EXPLORE: Musical Theatre Emotional Staircase
- *In the last lesson, we explored how music has this amazing way of conveying feelings. Today we're going to explore this a little further.*
- *In musicals there is an "emotional staircase" that exists. It has 3 steps, and characters move up the steps as their emotion heightens.*
- Draw the following on the board and explain each step in detail:

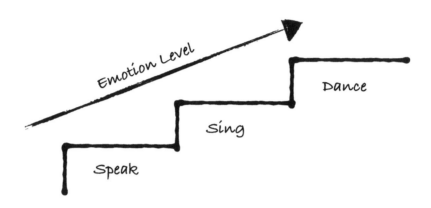

Step 1: Speak*
Just as in a regular play (or TV show or movie), characters have wants and intentions and they use dialogue and speech as a way to convey those wants.

Step 2: Sing
In a musical, characters move up the stairs to the next step, singing, when speaking isn't enough. Characters in a musical "break into song" because something happens that heightens the dramatic moment, and they are in a place of *more: more* intensity, *more* action, *more* wants, *more* needs. In some cases there are *more* obstacles working against them, *more* problems to solve, *more* resistance to overcome. (You can give examples from any of their favorite Disney movies.)

Step 3: Dance
This third step is when words fail the characters completely, and they must dance. The wordless, physical explosion of dance is a final attempt to communicate using every fiber of one's body. It's not enough to talk about something; it's not enough to sing about it. Now the character must try to embody the thing itself. (i.e. The scene where Beauty and the Beast dance together.)

* The above descriptions are adapted from Tracey Moore's *Acting the Song: Performance Skills for the Musical Theatre.*

EXPLORE: Newsies Clip

- *Let's take a look at this in action. I'm going to play a short clip from the Broadway production of Newsies.*
- Ask if anyone knows what the show is about. *Newsies tells the story of a group of young boys, mostly orphans and from poor families, who make ends meet by delivering newspapers in New York City in 1899. When they realize they are being taken advantage of by the large publisher, they decide to band together and do something about it: strike!* Play the clip.
- *What did you think about the performance?*
- *Did you see the characters move up the emotional staircase? Why do you think they began dancing?*
- *What qualities did the actors have that made the performance so entertaining?*
- Draw a stick figure on the board and list all the qualities with arrows coming from the stick figure.
- *These are skills we'll be working on as we train to be great musical actors.*

You can play any clip you'd like here that shows an energetic performance, but I highly recommend Newsies because the music and characters are relatable to young actors, and it will get even the "coolest" boys excited about singing and dancing.

If you happen to be using chart paper, save this sheet. It will come in handy for creating the performance rubric in Lesson 12.

ACTIVITY: Emotional Staircase Improv

- Give a funny improv example of moving up the emotional staircase: talking, then singing, then dancing. For example, you're watching TV with your friend to see if you've won the lottery (speech), the numbers are being drawn and you sing that this could finally be your chance (sing), you win the jackpot (dance!)
- Ask for volunteers, 2 at a time, to come up and improv their own progression up the staircase. Provide them with specific conflicts or ask the class for suggestions (i.e. Class starts in 5 minutes and your homework is due but you haven't even started yet. They should begin by talking, then singing, then dancing as the emotional level rises.
- Optional: You can play instrumental music to underscore their performance.
- *How did it feel as an actor? As an audience member?*

The story of Newsies is based on true events. If you'd like to go in more detail with your students about the strike, I've included a newspaper article excerpt on Page 64 in the bonus section.

REFLECTION

- *Drama Journal: Draw a picture of the emotional staircase.*
- *Newsies is a musical about a real historical event. Can you imagine an event from history that could inspire a musical? What would be the title of the hit song? Write it in your journal.*

Lesson 3: Music in Musicals (Part 1)

OBJECTIVE: Students will develop an understanding of how music is used to convey character and emotion, and how that understanding can help strengthen and inform their acting choices.

MATERIALS:

- Large writing surface
- 5 illustrations
- Music player with 5 contrasting instrumental music clips
- Make-shift musical instruments
- Story slips (see **Page 15**)

WARM-UP: Send the Clap

- Gather the group into a standing the circle.
- Send a clap around the circle (clockwise). Practice a couple times until everyone is focused and the clap has a natural rhythm.
- Ask if anyone knows the how to describe "loud" and "quiet" in music terms.
    - Loud = *Forte!* (pronounced: FOR-tay) Soft/quiet = *Piano*
- Have the class practice repeating these terms with the appropriate volume/energy, you could even add in a physical gesture
- Tell the class you'd like to send the clap around the circle again, but this time you want it to begin as *piano,* and gradually end as *FORTE!* (from quiet to loud)
- Repeat, but this time the opposite - gradually from *FORTE!* to *piano*
- Depending on the level of your students and available time, you could introduce the terms for fast and slow, and incorporate them into the commands for this activity:
    - Fast =*Vivace* (pronounced: vee-VAH-chay) Slow = *Adagio* (ah-DAH-gee-o)
        - *I'd like the clap to start as Vivace, and gradually end up as Adagio*
        - *I'd like the clap to start Adagio and Forte, then gradually become Vivace and Piano*
- Calm the energy by leading the class in a quick stretching exercise (see previous lesson)

> Feel free to swap the order of the physical warm-up and vocal warm-up from time to time. Sometimes if the group is high-energy in the beginning of class (which is often the case for after-school programs), I'll start with the vocal warm-up to calm them down and get them focused.

VOCAL WARM-UP:

- Tell everyone to sit lazy in their chairs like they're watching TV at home
- Then command *Ready to Sing!*
- Repeat the two vocal exercises from the previous lesson (High note to low note, Ha ha ha)
- Introduce the new one below:

Me_____ May_____ Mo Oh oh.   Me_____ May_____ Mo Oh oh.

Keep repeating a half-step higher, 6 or 7 more times.

EXPLORATION: Musical Colors

- *Who would like to share their drama journal "emotional staircase" assignment from the previous week?*
- In this class we're going to explore how music is used to tell stories in musicals, and the tools composers use to create music that supports the story and characters.
- This is important to us as actors, because if we have a deeper understanding of the music, we can pick up on little hints that could strengthen our performance.
- Just as painters use a combination of colors to make their artwork, composers also use what we're going to call "colors" of music to convey certain emotions.
- We talked about a few during the warm-up and we're going to explore a bunch more.
- Make a list of the following on the board and describe each one. Have the students repeat each term with you in a way that evokes what that term means. Depending on the age-level of the class, feel free to leave out any that you feel are too advanced.

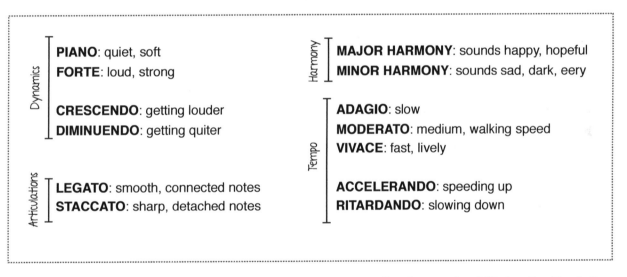

Dynamics

PIANO: quiet, soft
FORTE: loud, strong

CRESCENDO: getting louder
DIMINUENDO: getting quiter

Articulations

LEGATO: smooth, connected notes
STACCATO: sharp, detached notes

Harmony

MAJOR HARMONY: sounds happy, hopeful
MINOR HARMONY: sounds sad, dark, eery

Tempo

ADAGIO: slow
MODERATO: medium, walking speed
VIVACE: fast, lively

ACCELERANDO: speeding up
RITARDANDO: slowing down

- *Using the words from this chart, how would you describe the music of "Seize the Day", the video we watched in the last lesson?* Play a segment of the clip again if time permits.
- Write a list of their responses:
  - *Forte! Staccato! Vivace! Yes, great job.*
- *Why do you think the composer chose these "colors"? (Because the characters need to show strength and excitement.)*

ACTIVITY: Music Match

- Take out 5 illustrations/pictures, large enough for the whole class to see. These could be from picture books or other sources. The only consideration is that each should evoke a slightly different emotion.
- Place the illustrations in a row on the board. Briefly discuss the types of emotions each illustration evokes.
- Explain that you are going to play 5 short music samples, call them songs A through E, and they must match each one to an image.

> Before playing the music you may consider writing down agreed upon "colors" you'll be looking out for below each image For younger classes you could consider using only 3 examples.

ACTIVITY: Story Soundtrack

- Divide the class into 5 groups.
- Give each group a set of instruments. Ideally you could borrow a box of percussion instruments from your music teacher before class (shakers, drumsticks, tambourines, wood blocks, etc.) If you don't have access to music instruments, you could use children's toy instruments, or just everyday objects that make sound (cups, plastic spoons, books, etc.)

> For younger students, you can do this as a class activity.

- Give each group one of the illustrations and a blank "story slip" (see next page)
- They have 10 minutes to come up with a short story based on the illustration. One person from the group will be the "storyteller" while the rest of the group will use the sound from their instruments to provide the soundtrack.
- On the blank story slip they should summarize the beginning, middle and end of their story with the corresponding "colors of music" they have chosen. The "colors of music" should match the emotional content of the story.
- For very young actors, you can play the role of the storyteller while the kids use the instruments to accompany your story.
- Have each group share and explain their musical choices.
- Reflect: *Was that easy or difficult to do? Why?*

REFLECTION:

- *In what ways do composers use music to tell stories?*
- *Drama Journal: Write down your favorite song (from the radio, or from a movie). Describe the music using the "musical colors" we learned about today. Write down why you think those colors were chosen?*

Story Slips

Story Title:

	BEGINNING	MIDDLE	END
Story			
Musical Colors			

<u>Musical Colors:</u> *Piano, Forte, Crescendo, Diminuendo, Legato, Staccato, Major Harmony, Minor Harmony, Adagio, Moderato, Vivace, Accelerando, Ritardando*

Story Title:

	BEGINNING	MIDDLE	END
Story			
Musical Colors			

<u>Musical Colors:</u> *Piano, Forte, Crescendo, Diminuendo, Legato, Staccato, Major Harmony, Minor Harmony, Adagio, Moderato, Vivace, Accelerando, Ritardando*

Lesson 4: Music in Musicals (Part 2)

OBJECTIVE: Students will continue their understanding of how to let the music inform their acting choices.

MATERIALS:

- Music player
- Song clip: Opening theme to 2001: A Space Odyssey (https://youtu.be/VxLacN2Dp6A)
- "My Treehouse" Vocal Sheet Music (see **Page 18**)

PHYSICAL WARM-UP: Send the Clap, Part 2

- In a standing circle, repeat the "Send the Clap" game that you introduced in the last lesson.
- However this time include all the "colors of music" that the students learned (see **Page 13**).
- Ask a few volunteers to act as the "conductor" or "composer", instructing the group on which musical "colors" to use when sending the clap around.
- Lead a short stretching exercise.

VOCAL WARM-UP

- Have the class seated in *Ready to Sing* posture
- Repeat a few of the vocal warm-ups from the previous lessons
- Introduce pronunciation exercises:
  - *Stretch your face as big as possible for 5 seconds. 5… 4…3…2…1. Now make your face as tiny as possible for 5 seconds. 5…4…3…2…1. Now repeat after me: The lips! (they repeat) The teeth! (they repeat) The tip of the tongue! (they repeat) The lips, the teeth, the tip of the tongue! (they repeat)*
  - Repeat a few more times.

> As you continue with vocal warm-ups, occasionally you can call out individual names to allow the students the chance to sing solo. Or you can call out "first row only", or "only those wearing brown shoes", etc to keep focus and make it a game. This will also help you identify students who may need extra attention. Take the time to help those students who are off-pitch. Keeping the environment light and fun, work with them to "sing higher" with you, to one-on-one, try and match your pitch. Sometimes it is challenging for students to hear their own voice when singing in a group.

EXPLORE

- Ask a few students to share their drama journal entries from the previous lesson on the colors of their favorite song.
- Last week we explored how music is used in musicals. Today we're going to step on stage and explore what that feels like as actors

ACTIVITY: Slow Motion Pantomime

- *In this activity we're going to let the music affect how we perform an action on stage.*
- Play the music clip: Theme from 2001 A Space Odyssey (https://youtu.be/VxLacN2Dp6A)

- *I will be dividing the class into pairs. It is your job to come up with a very boring task (washing a window, doing the dishes, making a bed, weeding the garden, etc.)*
- *Your goal is for you and your partner to create an overly dramatic, epic scene in slow motion that centers around that task. The scene should have a beginning, middle, and end. This is a silent scene that will be accompanied by the music you are hearing now.*
- *You have 5 minutes to work on this with your partner.*
- Play the music as the partners work together.
- Allow the students to present their scenes, commending those that are focused and have a clear beginning, middle and end.

ACTIVITY: "My Treehouse" Song Transition

- Pass out the "My Treehouse" vocal sheet music (see **Page 18**)
- Explain to the class: *In this activity we're going to begin the practice of acting with music while transitioning into song. We will be learning a short monologue and the first verse of a song. You will learn how to listen to the music to transition from speaking to singing seamlessly.*
- *With an accompanist, perform the monologue and the first verse of the song. (The piano-vocal sheet music is included on* **Page 61***. You can hear a professionally recorded version of this song here:* https://youtu.be/n698mBAF_N8 *"Song for Kids: My Treehouse")*

> The song "My Treehouse" is from a Beat by Beat musical called The Most Epic Birthday Party Ever. This character, Skyler, has been planning her birthday party for months. But it suddenly becomes ruined when his/her older brother steals the spotlight. She runs up to her treehouse and sings this song.

- Teach the class the first verse of the song.
- Play the vocal track again and point out the "bell" that occurs 2 bars before the singing begins.
- The goal is to make the transition from speaking to singing seamless.
- Allow the students a few minutes of time to practice the monologue and first verse on their own.
- Then play the piano accompaniment and allow the class to practice as a group.
- Then call up individual students to perform the monologue/first verse in front of the class.

REFLECTION

- *How did it feel to be speaking a monologue with music underneath you?*
- *Was it easy or hard? Did it help you focus or distract you?*
- *Drama Journal: This week write down one time when you notice music in a television show or movie that really enhances the story. Describe it in detail.*

My Treehouse

SKYLER:
When I was 8 and was afraid to go to my first piano recital, I hid in this treehouse. I felt safe.
When I was 10 and my dad yelled at me for lying, this is where I ran to. I felt protected.
And now that I'm 12, and everyone has left me on my birthday...well, what better place to be?

Just me up here in my tree-house.

[End of Verse 1]

Not much to fear in my tree-house.   I'm all a-lone but I feel I be long here.

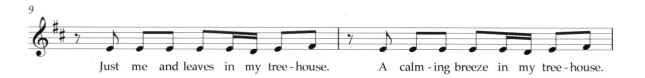

Just me and leaves in my tree-house.   A calm-ing breeze in my tree-house.

It may sound sim-ple,   but I can't do much wrong here. 'Cause in my tree

free-dom reigns.   So much to see a-bove the plains. Just lit-tle me, no

one com-plains.   So safe and sound in my tree-house,

I won't be found in my tree-house.   Un-less I want to be.

Lesson 5: Singing Musical Theatre (Part 1)

OBJECTIVE: Students will develop an understanding of how the voice works and basic vocal technique as it relates to singing musical theatre.

MATERIALS:
- Ball (a soft one that it can be easily passed around)
- Balloon
- Large writing surface

GREETING:
- Ask who can recap so far what we've learned about musical theatre?
- Ask a few volunteers to share their drama journal entry about where they noticed music was played in TV/film to enhance the story
- *Today we begin the in-depth exploration of proper singing technique. But first, some warm-ups!*

WARM-UP: Sound Ball
- Gather the class into a standing circle.
- Take out a round, soft ball.
- Ask: *If we had to turn this ball into a sound our mouth makes, what might it sound like?*
- *Ooohhh.*
- Move the ball in a circle, and have them move their heads and voices reflecting the ball's movement.
- *What do you think this balls sounds like when I throw it up in the air?*
- Give it a toss. Their voices should go up high and back down along with the ball.
- Pass the ball around the circle. Each student must give the ball a toss straight up and match the sound with their own voice.
- *Remember, the higher you throw it, the higher you have to sing!*

EXPLORE: How the Voice Works
- Have the class take a seat and ask the following questions:
  - *Who here enjoys singing?*
  - *Does anyone know how the voice works?*
  - *How were we able to make the sounds we did throwing the ball up in the air?*
  - *Has anyone ever lost their voice because of screaming too much at a sporting event or a concert? Does anyone know how or why that happens?*
  - *Today we're going to explore all these questions. As musical theatre actors we rely greatly on our voice to sing the songs and to tell the stories. We must understand how to sing properly and take care of our voice so we are able to perform over and over*

19

again. Most Broadway actors perform a 3-hour musical 8 times a week! It's crucial they, and all great musical actors, understand how to maintain a healthy voice.

• Ask if there is a volunteer who can demonstrate how to properly pitch a baseball.

• Ask him to come in front of the class to demonstrate.

• After doing it in real-time, ask him to do it in super-slow-motion.

• Ask the class: *Did he use his whole body, or just his arm?*

• Ask the volunteer: *Why didn't you just use your arm? Ohh, because you can throw much stronger? And have more control?*

• *Our voice works the same way - it requires the whole body to sing with strength and control.*

• *We're going to break this down into 3-simple stages.* Write the following on the board with the accompanying diagram and briefly discuss each stage.

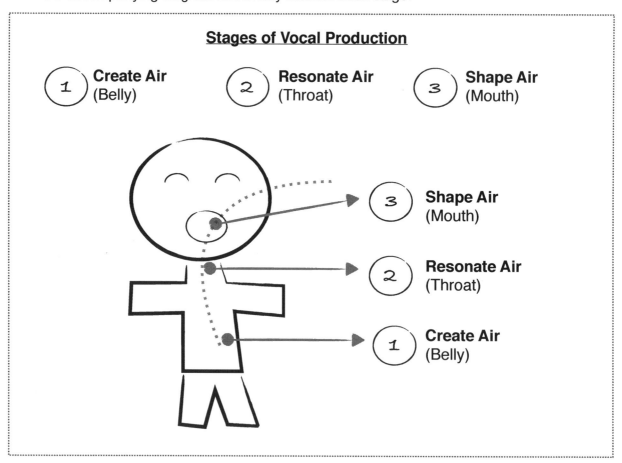

Stages of Vocal Production

1. **Create Air** (Belly)
2. **Resonate Air** (Throat)
3. **Shape Air** (Mouth)

3. **Shape Air** (Mouth)
2. **Resonate Air** (Throat)
1. **Create Air** (Belly)

ACTIVITY: Exploring Stage 1 - Breathing on the Floor

• *We're going to begin by focusing on Stage 1, creating the air, or breathing. Great vocal sound begins with great breath control.*

• Ask the class to spread out and find a place on the floor where they can lie down on their backs comfortably.

• Tell them to relax their shoulders and head, and to take deep breaths.

- *What part of your body moves when you take a deep breath?*
- *The belly! That muscle directly below your rib cage that is expanding in and out is called the diaphragm. When singing correctly air should always be coming from your diaphragm. It should constantly be expanding and compressing.* (You can remind them of the "Ha Ha Ha" vocal warm-up that utilizes the same muscle)
- Have them take a deep breath and let out an "Oooooooh" from high to low. They should feel their diaphragm getting smaller as they let out the sound.
- Now have them try the same thing *without* moving their *bellies. Notice the change in sound quality? Notice the strain in your throat? This is the incorrect way to sing. This is how you end up losing your voice!*

ACTIVITY: Exploring Stage 1 - Balloon Demonstration
- Have the class take a seat.
- Take out a deflated balloon. If possible place a small plastic mouth piece in the opening so it's easier to fill up with air.
- Explain that your diaphragm acts a lot like this balloon, and you're going to demonstrate how the size of your breath really affects how much sound you can produce.
- Take a small breath, and fill the balloon. Discuss.
- Take a giant breath, and fill the balloon. Notice the difference. *With the amount of air in this balloon I can reach the back of a Broadway theatre or hold a note longer than anyone else.*
- Give the class a starting pitch, and have them practice big breaths holding the note as long as possible on the vowel "Ahh".
- Optional: You can turn this into a game. Have them stand, give them the starting note, count 3, 2, 1, Go! When they run out of breath, they should sit down. Tell them you'll be monitoring their bellies to make sure they don't cheat. If it comes down to 2 or 3 students, pair them off for a final showdown.

ACTIVITY: Vocal Roller Coaster
- Have the class take a seat and remind them of *Ready to Sing* posture.
- Referring back to the Stages of Vocal Production Diagram, explain that we just covered Stage 1. *We sit in "Ready to Sing" posture so that after the air is created from your diaphragm, is passes effortlessly up through your vocal cords where it resonates, Stage 2. This allows it to have a direct line up and out of your mouth. Think of a garden hose that is tangled as opposed to one that is laid out straight—the water can flow much more easily when there are no obstructions. With the right breath control, and the right posture, we can sing notes we never thought imaginable! I'll show you what we mean with a little game called Vocal Roller Coaster.*
- Either on the board or a separate writing surface, explain you're an engineer who's going to create a roller coaster that their voice will take a ride on.

- Give the class the first note to start on and have the entire class "move" their voices up and down the roller coaster (You can choose any vowel sound).
- You can begin with simple designs like this:

- Then add loops:

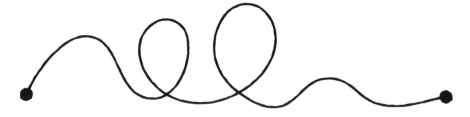

- Then you can even add stilts, so that they must start the ride on a higher note:

- If time permits, consider passing out blank pieces of paper and allowing each student to create his/her own roller coaster to present to the class.

ACTIVITY: Teach Remainder of "My Treehouse"
- *Let's put all these new skills into practice with a real song.*
- Pass out the vocal sheet to "My Treehouse" (**Page 18**). Teach the 2nd verse and bridge.
- Perform as a group, then as solos, giving feedback along the way.

REFLECTION:
- *Who can remind me of the 3 stages of vocal production?*
- *In the next class we will be focusing on the 3rd stage - shaping the sound.*
- *Drama Journal: What other jobs other than a singer/actor would benefit from knowing proper voice technique? List them in your journal.*

Lesson 6: Singing Musical Theatre (Part 2)

OBJECTIVE: Students will continue their exploration of proper singing technique with a focus on articulators (shaping the sound).

WARM-UP: Say Your Name
- Have the class stand in a circle.
- Explain that you are going to go around the circle, one by one, each student must say his/her name loudly. However, you cannot move your lips. *Go!*
- After one complete round, try again, but this time your tongue cannot touch your teeth. *Go!*
- Reflect: *Was this difficult? Why?*

EXPLORE: Articulation
- *Today we're continuing our exploration of proper singing technique.*
- *Last lesson we focused on creating the air and resonating the sound. Today we're focusing the on the 3rd stage, shaping the sound. We call this articulation. Proper articulation is important in musical theatre because the audience must be able to clearly understand the lyrics being sung. Remember, musical theatre songs often move the story forward and the lyrics contain important character information. Unlike a pop song, the audience can't pause and repeat a section if they want to hear it again. So we must make sure the words are clear the first time!*
- *As we discovered in the warm-up, we often take for granted how important our lips, teeth and tongue are for communicating clearly!*
- *Repeat after me: The lips! (class repeats) The teeth! (class repeats) The tip of the tongue! (class repeats) Repeat this all together a few times. Try saying it 3 times, loud and fast.*
- *We're now going to do some vocal warm-ups with a focus on articulation.*

Below I've listed some of my favorite vocal warm-ups for articulation divided into two categories:
1) Warm-ups appropriate for young actors
2) Warm-ups appropriate for older actors
Feel free to pick and choose based on what you think you and your students will enjoy the most!

VOCAL WARM-UPS FOR YOUNGER ACTORS

Big Face/Small Face/Cow (non-music)
- Have the class make their face as big as possible for 5 seconds
- Have the class make their face as tiny as possible for 5 seconds
- Have the class pretend they are a cow chewing grass, slowly and deliberately

Boat Sounds (non-music)

- This fun activity lets young kids explore different kinds of boat sounds while warming up their lips, teeth and tongue. Feel free to write these up on the board, or just have the class repeat after you.
    - **Police Boat:** *Whee-wooo-whee-wooo-whee-whoo* (like a siren)
    - **Tugboat:** *Toot toot! Chugga chugga. Toot toot! Chugga chugga.*
    - **Sailboat:** *Shhhhhhhh…Clink! Clank! Flap flap flap. Clink! Clank! Flap flap flap.*
    - **Paddle Boat:** *Chum, Splish! Chum, Splash!*
    - **Speed Boat:** *Grrrrrrrrrrr…wrrrrrrrrrrr…grrrrrrrrrrrrr!* (crescendoing each time)
    - **Submarine:** *Bing! Nnnnnnnnnn. Bing! Nnnnnnnnn.*
- Encourage kids to really exaggerate each and every sound.
- You can also make it a game by quickly pointing to different boats on the board or ask volunteers to come up one by one to demonstrate.

Mama Made Me Mash My M&M's, Oh My!

- With the vocal warm-up below you can add the physical gesture of the kids pounding M&M's, with one fist lightly pounding into an open palm.

Keep repeating a half-step lower, 6 or 7 more times.

Super Duper Double Bubble Gum

Keep repeating a half-step higher, 6 or 7 more times.

VOCAL WARM-UPS FOR OLDER ACTORS

> Every so often ask the class to do the warm-ups in different styles: i.e. Like a rock star! Like an opera singer. Like a wicked witch. etc.

Tongue Twisters

- A bragging baker baked black bread.
- A proper copper coffee pot.
- Smelly shoes and socks shock sisters.
- For a full list of tongue twisters, see **Page 57** under bonus material.

24

Po Po Ka Ta Petal

- Write the following syllables on the board: *Po Po Ka Ta Petal.* Have the class repeat them with you until they are comfortable, then add the music:

Po po ka ta pe-tal Po po   ka ta pe-tal Po po ka ta   pe-tal Po po ka ta pe-tal   Po.

Keep repeating a half-step higher, 5 or 6 more times.

Bumble Bee

Bum - ble - bee____   Bum - ble - bee____   Bum - ble - bee____   Bum - ble - bee.

Bum - ble - bee____   Bum - ble - bee____   Bum - ble - bee____   Bum - ble - bee.

Keep repeating a half-step higher, 4 or 5 more times.

ACTIVITY: Singing Vowels

- Ask students to list all the vowels of the alphabet.
- Write them up on the board, from top to bottom.
- Explain that when we sing, vowels have a slightly different sound than when we read. This is to produce a more full, resonant sound that's more pleasant to the ear.
- Write the "singing vowels" next to the original vowels, as in the chart below:

A	=	Ah
E	=	Eh
I	=	Ee
O	=	Oh
U	=	Oo

- Give a starting pitch, then sing through each "singing vowel" in long, drawn out notes.

- You can use the following warm-up to practice:

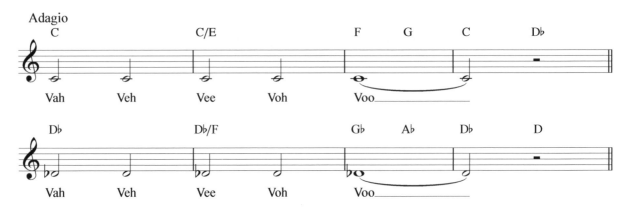

Keep repeating a half-step higher, 6 or 7 more times.

- Explain that the larger the opening of the mouth, the bigger the sound. You can highlight this point if you have a megaphone handy, and using it both ways to show the difference in sound production. You can also use a rubber band on the outside of your fingers to highlight the proper shape of the mouth and how it changes with each vowel sound.

ACTIVITY: Go 'Way From My Window:

- You can practice these vowel sounds with the short song below:

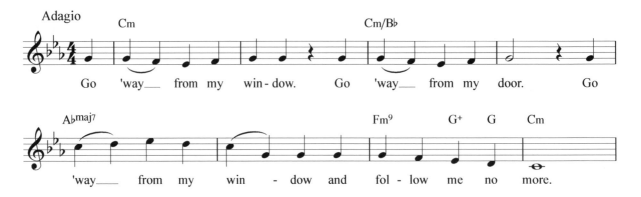

ACTIVITY: Song Work

- Continue work on "My Treehouse" teaching the rest of the song keeping in mind these new skills and techniques

REFLECTION:

- *Drama Journal: Search for one of your favorite musical theatre songs on YouTube and find one great performance and one poor performance. Describe them in your journal.*

Lesson 7: Dance & Movement (Part 1)

OBJECTIVE: Students will explore how dance and movement contribute to storytelling in musical theatre. They will also become comfortable and familiar with basic choreography.

MATERIALS:
- Audio clip of "One" from *A Chorus Line* Karaoke Track (https://youtu.be/2YtZHaI6li0)

WARM-UP: Practice With 8-Counts
- This warm-up will help students become familiar with the idea of 8-counts in choreography.
- Have the class stand and fill up the empty space of the stage, facing you.
- Play the instrumental audio clip of "One" from A Chorus Line (after it gets to minute 2:20 you'll want to repeat from the beginning again)
- Explain that everyone is to mirror your dance movements.
- Improvise a sequence for 8-counts, then stand still for 8-counts.
- Make sure you're counting loudly throughout: *1, 2, 3, 4, 5, 6, 7, 8!* (You can count loudly when dancing, quietly when standing still.)
- Explain that in musical choreography, dance movements are typically broken up into 8-counts.
- Have the class split into two, each group standing on either side of the stage.
- Keep the music playing.
- Explain that when you say "next" one person from each group must enter the center area and together improvise a dance. They must alternate 8-counts - which means Student A dances for 8-counts, then Student B dances for 8-counts. (For younger kids you can help demonstrate in the beginning)
- Count out loud and help cue the students.
- Once the class has become comfortable with the activity, call out an emotion that the actors must reflect in their dance.

EXPLORE: Dance & Movement in Musicals
- Have the class take a seat.
- Remind the students that musical theatre is a "heightened" form of telling stories, and one tool that adds to this heightened form is dance.
- Remind the students of the 3 steps of emotion in musical theatre (see **Page 10**)
- Explain that all movement in musical theatre has a purpose. It can:
    1. Express emotion
    2. Advance the plot
    3. Give deeper understanding of character/conflict
- Ask for students to give examples of how each purpose might be used.

- Ask the students to recall the video clip they watched earlier in the semester of "Seize the Day"? Which one of these purposes was used?
- If time permits, consider showing a video of the opening dance sequence of *West Side Story*. Have the class describe the action and how they knew what was happening. This is an example of using dance to further the plot.
- Explain that standing motionless may be appropriate in dramatic plays and film/TV, but in musicals having some sort of purposeful action/movement is almost always a stronger choice. It helps punctuate emotions, and can bring new perspectives to character relationships.

ACTIVITY: Choreography Formations

- *Now lets learn some basic choreography tools that will help us create visually exciting stage pictures.*
- Have the class take the stage.
- Tell the students you are going to be teaching them a series of commands. They should move to their spots quickly and silently.
    - *Fill:* everyone should spread themselves evenly on the stage, facing the audience.
    - *Clump:* students should all clump in the middle of the stage, facing the audience.
    - *2 Clumps:* students should form 2 even clumps
    - *3 Clumps:* students should form 3 even clumps

  Consider playing uptempo music during this activity.

- *Next we're going to learn levels:*
    - *Low:* students should strike a pose that is low to the ground
    - *Medium:* students should strike a pose that is mid-height
    - *High:* students should strike a "high" pose
- Try all these commands out, then mix and match. Say *Clump, Low* then *3 Clumps, High.*
- Then instruct the students in the front of the clump to strike a *Low* pose, middle of the clump strike a *Medium* pose, back of the clump strike a *High* pose.
- You should now have a beautiful stage tableaux, with minimal instruction!
- Now onto lines:
    - *1 Line:* 1 horizontal line across the stage
    - *2 Lines:* 2 even horizontal lines, one in front, one in back
    - *3 Lines:* 3 even horizontal lines
    - *V:* a V shape, with the tip upstage
    - *Semi-Circle:* a semi-circle that bends upstage
- Then ask for *1 Line.* Have students count off down the line "Zig", "Zag", "Zig", "Zag", etc.
- Instruct: *If you're a Zag, please take 2 steps back.*
- You've now just created two staggered lines, with "windows" for each student in the back. Magic!

ACTIVITY (Optional): Choreography Steps

- If you have the experience, now would be the time to continue introducing other basic dance steps such a box step, step-ball-change, etc.
- There are many YouTube video examples for these basic moves that can demonstrate these steps better than I can describe here.
- Arrange the students into 2 lines, have them "Zig, Zag", then lead them through the moves you'd like them to become familiar with.
- Every so often rotate the lines: Have the back line come to the front, and the other lines move back.

ACTIVITY: Choreograph a Song

- Choreograph a song you've been working on using the dance/movement commands above. (A short section of "Seize the Day" from *Newsies* is a great option.)
- Remind the students that just as in the video they watched of "Seize the Day", every movement should be crisp, clear and confident.

REFLECTION:

- *Why is dance/movement important in musicals?*
- *Drama Journal: Find a book in your backpack and write down the 3rd sentence of the 1st chapter. Create an original 8-count dance inspired by that sentence.*

Lesson 8: Dance & Movement (Part 2)

OBJECTIVE: Students will add to their choreography toolkit, then use that toolkit to create original choreography and share it with the class.

MATERIALS:
- Music player

GREETING: Who would like to share their original 8-count from the Drama Journal activity? Allow a few students to present their dance.

WARM-UP: Copycat Dance
- Have the students stand in a circle
- Play some upbeat music.
- Choose one student to enter the circle and begin some repetitive dance movement
- That student then chooses someone from the circle and goes directly in front of him/her. The chosen student then copycats the movement, and they trade places so the new student is now in the middle.
- The new student must change the dance move slightly, then repeat the process again.
- Continue until everyone has had a chance to be in the middle.
- Calm the energy of the class by doing some breathing/stretching exercises.

> As the class watches, you can have them participate by either clapping to the beat, or chanting "Go Ryan! Go Ryan!" for each student in the middle.

VOCAL WARM-UP:
- Choose 1 articulation warm-up and 2 vocal warm-ups from previous lessons (or consult **Pages 58-59** in the Bonus Section).

EXPLORATION: Movement
- Have the class take a seat
- Place 2 chairs facing each other on the stage
- Ask 2 volunteers to come up and sit in the chairs
- These two actors will improvise a scene. Actor A is the big boss of a newspaper company, and Actor B is a newsie asking for a raise
- Here's the catch: They must perform this scene knees-to-knees facing each other, looking straight into each other's eyes. They cannot move at all.
- Reflect:
  - To the actors:
    - *How difficult was it to act without moving?*
    - *What would have made it easier?*

> Feel free to substitute this situation for anything that has two characters with opposing wants. I chose Newsies to stick with a familiar theme.

- To the audience:
    - *What was it like to watch the scene? Did it feel natural?*
    - *Was it interesting to watch?*
- Ask for 2 more volunteers to come up, however this time they must improvise the same scene in the *opposite* way. They must travel somewhere different onstage for each line.
- Reflect:
    - *What did the scene feel like? Did this seem natural? Was it distracting?*
- Finally, ask for 2 more volunteers to perform the scene with complete freedom - they can move however they want.
- In musicals, movement and choreography is enhanced (or heightened), but always naturally motivated by the characters and what they want. The music, dialogue and lyrics should inform the movement.

ACTIVITY: Student-Led Choreography
- Review the dance formations and basic choreography from the previous class.
- Choose a song you've been working on, and divide the song into sections.
- Assign a group to each section. Their goal is to come up with original choreography for that section that reflects the music and lyrics.
- Give the groups 10 minutes.
- Have each group share their segment, then teach it to the class.
- Combine all the segments together in a cohesive number.

Tips for Successful Student Choreography

- List all the steps/formations on the board that the students have learned
- Suggest they also incorporate any steps they have learned from previous learning (an outside dance academy, other training, etc.)
- Remind the class that all students don't have to be dancing at the same time. Dancers can be added in or groups can alternate.
- If they are having trouble deciding who is in charge, encourage them to have each student in the group be in charge of one 8-count

REFLECTION:
- Which groups' choreography seemed the most natural? *Why?*
- What were some of the challenges of creating your own choreography?
- *Drama Journal: Answer this question: What style of choreography do you most enjoy watching? What style do you most enjoy performing? Why?*

Lesson 9: Acting the Song (Part 1)

OBJECTIVE: Students will explore the importance of "acting a song" as opposed to just performing a song. They will begin to integrate the skills they've learned so far into a cohesive, authentic performance.

MATERIALS:
- The lyrics of the song "Strong" from *The Lightning Thief* copied and pasted onto a sheet to look like dialogue. You'll read more about this activity below. You can find the lyrics here (https://goo.gl/XyFbFA)
- Audio clip of "Strong" from *The Lightning Thief* (https://youtu.be/83aLKTNc0Jo)

VOCAL WARM-UP
- Choose 1 articulation warm-up and 2 vocal warm-ups from previous lessons (or consult **Pages 58-59** in the Bonus Section)

PHYSICAL WARM-UP: Cold Read
- Tell the class that instead of a typical physical warm-up today we're going to warm-up by doing a cold-read of a two person scene.
- The scene you'll be giving them will actually be lyrics from a lesser-known musical, but don't tell them that!
- For this activity I recommend using the song "Strong" from the musical *The Lightning Thief: Percy Jackson Musical.* You can find the lyrics here: https://goo.gl/XyFbFA
- You'll want to copy/paste the lyrics into a document and take out any (sung) or (speak) stage directions. I also recommend changing the character names to something generic. The idea is for it to look like a script from a play, like below:

> *If students aren't familiar with the term "cold-read", explain that it's when an actor performs something without any rehearsal.*

MOM: I can't tell you all my secrets.

SON: Maybe you should start with one.

MOM: You're right...I'll show you where I met your dad. He'd be proud of his son.

SON: Who cares? We're better off without him.

- Explain that this is scene between a mother and son - the son's father just happens to be Poseidon. (If for some reason they figure it out this is Percy Jackson - just say yes, it's from a new play based on the books/movie.)

> *As a reminder, you can use any duet here – as long as the song is not instantly recognizable.*

- Ask a few pairs of volunteers to come up and read the scene in front of the class.
- Reveal that these are actually song lyrics from a musical.
- Play the audio recording of the song, allowing the students to follow along.
- *What did you notice?*
- *In musical theatre, acting a song is just as important as singing a song. It's helpful at times to think of song lyrics as a straight scene, to never lose sight of the story.*

EXPLORATION: Acting a Song

- With the class seated, explore further the idea of acting a song:
  - *One of the most important aspects of musical theatre performance that a beginning student must understand is that when you begin singing, you <u>do not</u> stop acting. This may seem obvious - but it's one of the easiest things to forget. Unlike when performing at a local talent show or concert, in musical theatre the song is always coming from a specific character in a specific situation with specific wants. The music and lyrics must appear to be coming from the character in real-time - it should feel like it's being created and thought of in <u>that specific moment.</u>*
  - *The exercises we're going to be doing for the next couple sessions are going to help us stay in the moment. We're going to practice how to better act a song.*

ACTIVITY: "My Treehouse" Review

- *We're going to be using the song "My Treehouse" to practice. Let's review it.*
- Hand out the "My Treehouse" song sheet and review it with the class. **(Page 18)**
- If you haven't already, lead a discussion with the class about the conflict that leads up to this song: Skyler has been planning and looking forward to her/his birthday party for months. When the day finally arrives everything goes terribly wrong. On top of all that, her friends ignore her and choose to hang out with his/her "cooler" brother instead.

ACTIVITY: Personalize the Song

- A first step to having students give an authentic performance is finding a way for them to personally connect with the song.
- Ask one brave student to take the stage and guide them through a series of questions to help them find a personal connection with the song. Here's an example of some guided questions:
  - *Have you ever been excited about a big event, but you were disappointed because it didn't go as planned?*
  - *What did it feel like?*
  - *If you're upset, do you have a place you like to go to? What place? Why? How does it make you feel to be there?*
  - *Have you ever felt jealous of someone?*
  - *How do you calm yourself down if you feel angry?*
  - *What's been the best birthday you've ever had? The worst?*

33

- Have them perform with that new connection.
- Have the rest of the class write down one personal connection they have with what Skyler is feeling.

ACTIVITY: Perform the Song
- Ask a few students to come up and perform the song with that strong personal connection in mind. Remind them to take into account proper singing technique, and natural stage movement that feels authentic
- Give the following feedback for each performer:
  - *I really enjoyed how you* _____
  - *I wonder if it might be stronger if you* _____

REFLECTION:
- What did it feel like to focus on acting and singing at the same time?
- What do you think it would feel like if you also had to focus on dancing?
- *Drama Journal: Write down one song that you think you would really enjoy being able to sing and act.*

Lesson 10: Acting the Song (Part 2)

OBJECTIVE: Students will continue their understanding of how to interpret a song with a focus on song structure, intent and movement.

MATERIALS:
- An empty picture frame

WARM-UP: 10 Dollars, Please
- Gather the students into a circle, with you the instructor standing in the middle.
- One by one, the students are going to try and convince you to lend them 10 dollars.
- But every so often your "character" is going to change.
- Begin as their best friend, choose a student to start, and say *Go!* When you say *Next* the next student in the circle should begin.
- Every so often you'll change your character. Here is a list of characters you can become:
  - *I am now...*
    - *your younger cousin in kindergarten*
    - *your father*
    - *your favorite teacher*
    - *your least favorite teacher*
    - *your 85-year old grandma*
    - *your angry older brother*
    - *a stranger*
    - *your worst enemy*
    - *your crush*
    - *etc.*
- *What was that warm-up like? What did you notice? How did your tactic change based on who you were speaking to?*
- *When performing a song, two of the most important questions you can ask are:*
  1. *What do I want?*
  2. *Who am I speaking to?*
- We're going to focus on these two questions today, but first, let's warm-up our voices.

VOCAL WARM-UP:
- Choose 1 articulation warm-up and 2 vocal warm-ups from previous lessons (or consult **Pages 58-59** in the Bonus Section)

EXPLORE: Who Am I Singing To?
- Introduce an empty picture frame. Explain that this frame will represent whomever you are singing the song to.
- In the song "My Treehouse" who are you talking to?
- Many students will answer "myself".
- Explain that while "myself" can be true, often times that leads to a very small, closed performance. Let's explore some other imaginary options:
- Ask a volunteer to take the stage.

- Ask the volunteer who her best friend is.
- Explain that you want the volunteer to imagine her best friend is in the empty picture frame. This friend is seeing this treehouse for the first time and just asked, "Why are you up here?"
- Have the volunteer perform the song, immediately from this moment, as if she's singing to her best friend who's in the picture frame.
- Ask the rest of the class, *How did the performance change? What specifically did you notice that was different?*
- *Was it more interesting to watch? Why?*
- Explain that by imagining you're singing to another character, it "opens up" the scene—it makes it much more "alive".
- If it doesn't make sense to imagine singing to someone else, another option is to sing to a "version" of yourself. For example, *You could imagine that inside that picture frame is a really sad version of yourself, and you are trying hard to cheer her up.* Although this sounds a little "high-level", you'll be amazed at how this can bring new life to a performance that is beginning to feel a little rote.
- Ask every student to write in their journal 3 possible people to whom they could be singing the song.
- If time allows, ask a few more volunteers to perform with one of their choices inside the picture frame.

ACTIVITY: Sing with the Eyes
- *Now that we understand the importance of directing a song "toward" someone, this next activity will help us keep that focus throughout the whole performance.*
- Optional: At this point, you can consider showing the class a YouTube video of a poor musical theatre solo performance, in which the actor is not engaged or focused. You can ask the class: *What did you think? Why?* Responses may vary, but they should have something to do with: it didn't capture my attention, it was boring, the actor wasn't focused.

> If you want to show the class an example of an actor who is incredible at acting through his eyes, search YouTube for performances by Ben Funkhauser.

- Explain that as humans, the majority of our communication comes from our face and eyes. To give an authentic performance, we need to make sure we are "singing through our eyes".
- Place 5 chairs on the stage, and choose 5 students to come sit in them.
- Tell them that you're going to play the vocal track for "My Treehouse" and they need to perform it using only their face and eyes. No other movement. (https://www.youtube.com/watch?v=n698mBAF_N8)
- If they break character or laugh, you will gently tap their shoulder and they must sit back in the audience.
- Tell the audience to carefully observe who is telling the story the best with their eyes.

ACTIVITY: "My Treehouse" Performances

- Allow a few students to perform "My Treehouse" (or any other song(s) you've been working on) solo, incorporating the picture frame and "singing with the eyes". Discuss any positive differences you've noticed.

REFLECTION:

- *What are 2 techniques you can use to improve your ability to act a song?*
- *Drama Journal: Make a list of 3 people in your life who would completely alter the way you performed the song if you were directing the song to one of them. (i.e. The school bully, etc.)*

Lesson 11: The Role of the Ensemble

OBJECTIVE: Students will learn how to become strong ensemble members by keeping scenes focused and creating an authentic "world" of the show.

MATERIALS:
- Old newspapers
- *Optional:* Short Newsies scene to precede "Seize the Day"

PHYSICAL WARM-UP: Join the World
- Have the class stand in a circle
- Explain to them that one student must enter the circle and begin some activity (for example, pretending to be a baseball player at bat)
- One-by-one the rest of the class must silently join the "world" of the activity by becoming a character that would authentically exist in this scene. For example, one student may become the pitcher, another the catcher, some could be fans in the stands, or a hotdog vendor, or a sports announcer, etc.
- The students should make an effort to fill the whole space of the stage so that it creates an interesting tableaux (stage picture) for the audience.
- Once the whole class has joined in, say "freeze" and walk around to assess how authentic the world is.
- Then reset, and begin a new round.
- Reflect:
  - *What were the challenges of this activity?*
  - *Was it easier to join in at the beginning or at the end?*
  - *What do you think this has to do with musical theatre?*

EXPLORE: The Role of the Ensemble
- Have the class take a seat.
- Explore: *In musicals the ensemble plays a very important and active role. Today we're going to focus on what skills are necessary to be a strong ensemble member.*
- First, ask the class to describe what they think are the qualities of a good ensemble member. (My favorite way to do any activity like this is to draw a stick figure on the board, then arrows coming out of her listing the suggestions. For this activity you might draw a group of little stick figures.) Sample answers may be:
  - *Lots of energy*
  - *Strong voices*
  - *Focused*
  - *Doesn't goof around*
  - *Pays attention to the story*
  - *Stays in character*
  - *etc.*
- Explain that a strong ensemble adds to the story and keeps a scene focused. Since

musicals tend to be more elaborate in production size than straight plays, it is up to the ensemble to help the audience know where to pay attention. The worst thing an ensemble member can do is take focus *away* from an important part of the story.

- Today we're going to all be come an ensemble in the hit Broadway show Newsies to setup the song "Seize the Day".

> You can compare this idea to film, where in big scenes usually only one or two characters are in focus at the same time, while the rest are blurred in the background.

ACTIVITY: World of Newsies

- Remind the class of the setting of Newsies: 1899 on the streets of New York City. (see **Page 64** for further background and context)
- Explain that in this activity, it's 5:30am - right before the work rush starts.
- Place stacks of newspapers on the stage.
- Ask to class to fill up the stage as Newsies. Just as in the warm-up activity, they should engage in some activity authentic to the world. This could include folding papers, counting money, getting dressed, eating breakfast, just waking up, etc.
- From the view of the audience it should create a beautiful and balanced stage picture.
- Tell the class for this activity you'll be using film terms, "Action" and "Cut".
- When you say "Action" the characters should come alive, 100% focused on the activity and the world they're living in.
- Call *Action* and *Cut* a few times to let them practice.
- Give notes along the way to help improve the stage picture.
- Encourage the students to use levels (like we practiced in Lesson 8) to help the audience see everything that is happening - lowest levels downstage, highest levels upstage. If you have stage blocks or chairs, consider adding them to help add texture.
- When things are looking good, tell the class you're going to call out a students' name, and the class should subtly direct their attention to that student. They shouldn't stop what they are doing, but simply turn their gaze.
- Practice this a few times, calling out different names. This is how they should act if someone has a line during a scene. They should help focus the audience's attention while remaining in character.
- Tell the class that you (the instructor) are now going to cross the scene as different types of characters. The class should react in an authentic way. Example characters could be:
  - A wealthy business person (they should try and sell you papers)
  - The boss of the newspaper company, who has been ripping them off

> Here are some other Newsies scenarios you can explore:
> - waiting in line to get your papers
> - you got your papers, but now you have a heavy bag on your shoulder and you're moving through a busy crowded street
> - you're hunting for a spot to sell papers
> - you're meeting with fellow Newsies after the rush
> - hunting for shelter from rain
> - running into rival Newsies competitors
> - hunting for safety from cops because maybe you stole your last meal

- The mayor of New York City
- A young kid who is always trying to mooch off the Newsies
- etc.
- If you've been rehearsing "Seize the Day", have this exploration activity lead into a performance of the song. Beforehand there should be a few lines from *Newsies* who are fed up with their low wages and ready to do something about it. You can write up a small scene beforehand to give to the students, or have them improvise the lead-in themselves.

ACTIVITY: World of Anything

- You can repeat this same activity to create other "worlds" that connect with the material you are working on.
- For example, you could create the world of a backyard birthday party to setup "My Treehouse"
- Have the class create a believable stage picture, pick an activity, use levels, and then call our students' names to practice adjusting focus. Those students could even improvise a line that's authentic to their character.

REFLECTION:

- *What's the most challenging part of being a strong ensemble member?*
- *Drama Journal: Write down 3 other things that require the work of the whole ensemble.*

A Note About Lessons 12-16

It's important to give students the chance to apply the skills they've learned into a public performance, even if it's just for family and friends. There are many different ways to put a "sharing" presentation together. The next 5 lessons will help guide you on activities you can do to help prepare your students.

These lessons can be spread out across as many weeks as needed to prepare your students for a successful performance. Don't feel you have to use these lessons "as is", but instead think of them as a guide as you prepare for your show.

I recommend an end-of-semester performance that allows students to participate both as an ensemble member and as a featured solo. This will provide them the most well-rounded experience to serve them in the next show they participate in. It will also allow those with natural talent (or hidden talent) the opportunity to improve and shine.

The performance material can be assigned and taught throughout the semester as you move through each lesson, or you can use the lessons to first create a strong base of skills, then focus on applying those skills to specific material later in the semester.

A Note About Shy Students

There may be a few students that are not comfortable performing a solo. Use every tool you can to encourage them to give it a try. Create the most supportive environment possible. They should feel there is no such thing as failure!

However if these shy students still feel uncomfortable and resistant, let them know that it's okay and they can just participate in the ensemble numbers. (*Maybe next year!*) Encourage them to still choose a solo number to practice on their own, but they won't be required to perform it by themselves in front of an audience. (Many times these shy students take the work very seriously and are fully prepared. They just don't have the confidence yet. And that's totally okay! You may want to consider keeping them after class toward the end of the semester and asking if they want to perform their number just for you - the instructor. You'll be amazed at what you see!)

A Note About Younger Students

If the students are very young (under 6), then individual solo songs are probably not necessary. You can simply assign short one-line solos as part of the group numbers.

Scenes Before Songs

A great way to include some scene-work is to create your own 1-2 page scene before each ensemble number. You can transcribe these scenes from YouTube videos or scripts that you purchase online. Try to include as many characters as you can, and have these characters assigned before you hand out the scenes.

Material for the Sharing Performance

For a class with limited time, it can become overwhelming if you allow every student to choose their own individual songs for solo performance. Instead, I feel it's more beneficial to have 3-4 solo songs that students can choose from, plus 2-3 ensemble numbers. By limiting the number of choices, it's makes the selection process easier for the students, plus they get the added benefit of watching the same material performed in many different ways by their peers. This serves as a great learning tool as it will open their eyes to a variety of performance choices. And with the help of your feedback as the instructor, they will be able to assess these choices with a critical eye.

You can also add a short monologue before each solo song, inspired by lines from the original musical script. This will allow the actor the chance to practice the "speaking to singing" transition.

You can source all the material from a single musical, or you can mix and match songs from different resources and present them in a "cabaret" type format.

To stick with the *Newsies* theme, here are songs I might prepare for my class:

- **3 Ensemble Numbers** *(Cut and arranged to be approximately 3 minutes)*
  - Carrying the Banner (optional solos in the beginning)
  - King of New York (optional solos in the beginning)
  - Seize the Day (optional solos in the beginning)
- **3 Solo Numbers** *(Cut and arranged to be no longer than 1 minute 30 seconds. Students will choose 1 of these to work on as a solo)*
  - Santa Fe
  - Watch What Happens
  - The World Will Know

Before printing the material, make sure it's in an appropriate key for the majority of your students. With digital music publishing websites, you can easily alter the key before printing. You can find the complete version of almost any musical theatre song on musicnotes.com. And if you need a little extra help finding appropriate cuts of the songs, performerstuff.com has a great selection of 16-bar and 32-bar versions of popular musical theatre songs.

At Beat by Beat Press, we offer a section called **Beat by Beat Singles** that includes material perfect for the sharing performance. Beat by Beat Singles are stand-alone songs for young performers ideal for musical theatre classes. These songs come arranged for young voices and are available through an instant download where you get the sheet music and full backing tracks.

You can browse the Beat by Beat Singles here:

http://www.bbbpress.com/songs-for-kids/

For an extensive list of musical theatre songs for young performers, check out this blog post:

https://goo.gl/otVS6n

Now, back to the lessons!

Lesson 12: Choosing a Song

OBJECTIVE: Students will begin to prepare for a small performance at the end of the semester by choosing a solo song and creating a performance rubric.

MATERIALS:
- Handouts of ensemble and solo songs for the students
- Large writing surface

GREETING:
- Tell the students *Congratulations! You have successful passed the audition process and have been cast in a Broadway show! From this point forward we're going to be working toward putting the show together, utilizing all the skills we've learned from the previous lessons.*

PHYSICAL WARM-UP: Circle Perfection
- Tell the class that you want them to create a standing circle, like they've done many times before.
- However this time, you want it to be a *perfect* circle. You will be standing up on a chair to assess this.
- You will give them 30 seconds.
- When they've completed the task, ask them to mix themselves up in the room, and create the perfect circle again, this time without using any words.
- Repeat one more time, this time in only 10 seconds.
- *How did you do? Did you improve with each repetition? What could have been done better?*
- Today we begin our rehearsal process and the secret to a good rehearsal is working well and efficiently together.

EXPLORE:
- Explain to the students what is expected of them for the performance at the end of the semester.
- Each student will participate in ensemble numbers in addition to a solo number.
- They will have [3] solo songs to choose from.
- *We will be presenting for a small group of family and friends.*
- *The final performance will be video-taped, and during the last class of this semester we will watch the tape to see how far we've come.*

ACTIVITY: Create Performance Rubric

- In order to measure our improvement it's important for us to know what goals we are striving toward.
- To help us do that we need to create a Performance Rubric. Explain that a rubric is sort of like a scoring guide to measure the quality of our performance. They are very helpful in keeping us focused as we rehearse.
- With the class seated, stand at the white board and ask the class to call out acting skills we've worked on so far this semester.
- Write them on the board. Group the responses into categories:
    - 1) Music & Voice
    - 2) Movement/Dance
    - 3) Acting the Song
    - 4) Ensemble
- Each item will be rated on a scale of 1 to 4, 1 being "Fair", and 4 being "Superior"
- Explain that we will be referring to this rubric throughout the rehearsal process.
- I've included a sample rubric that you can print and use on **Page 47.**

VOCAL WARM-UP:

- *Now let's turn our attention to the songs we'll be performing, but first let's warm-up our voices.*
- Choose 1 articulation warm-up and 2 vocal warm-ups from previous lessons (or consult **Page 58-59** in the Bonus Section)

ACTIVITY: Introduce Solo Songs

- For each song:
    - Describe the context and character
    - Perform the song for the students
- Explore some things the students may want to think about before choosing their solo song:
    - They should choose a song they connect with
    - They should choose a song they can become passionate about
- Tell the students to come up and grab the music to the song of their choice
- Teach each solo song to the group that chose it. Spend about 10-15 minutes with each group.
- When not participating, the other students should find a quiet spot and begin memorizing and practicing their song.

ACTIVITY: Introduce Ensemble Songs

- If time allows, begin teaching and working on the ensemble songs.

REFLECTION:

- *Have your solo song memorized by next week.*
- *Drama Journal: Answer these questions about your solo song choice:*
    - *Why am I singing this song?*

- *What two emotions am I feeling?*
- *Where am I?*
- *Who am I singing to?*
- *Is there a problem I need solved?*
- *What is my ideal solution to my problem?*

Musical Theatre Performance Rubric

1 = Fair 3 = Excellent 2 - Good 4 = Superior!	Name:	Name:	Name:	Name:
MUSIC & VOICE				
Music Transition Did the transition into song feel natural?	1 2 3 4	1 2 3 4	1 2 3 4	1 2 3 4
Projection & Diction Could you hear and understand the lyrics?	1 2 3 4	1 2 3 4	1 2 3 4	1 2 3 4
Vocal Variation Did they convey the emotion of the character with musical "colors"?	1 2 3 4	1 2 3 4	1 2 3 4	1 2 3 4
MOVEMENT/DANCE				
Eyes and Facial Gestures Did they use their face and eyes to express the character's emotion?	1 2 3 4	1 2 3 4	1 2 3 4	1 2 3 4
Movement Did they use movement to engage the audience?	1 2 3 4	1 2 3 4	1 2 3 4	1 2 3 4
ACTING THE SONG				
Character Want Could you tell what the character(s) wanted?	1 2 3 4	1 2 3 4	1 2 3 4	1 2 3 4
Authentic Did it feel like it was happening "in the moment"?	1 2 3 4	1 2 3 4	1 2 3 4	1 2 3 4
ENSEMBLE				
Was the ensemble focused and did they support the story?	1 2 3 4	1 2 3 4	1 2 3 4	1 2 3 4
NOTES:				

Lesson 13: Rehearsal

OBJECTIVE: Students will work on their ensemble and solos numbers in preparation for the final performance.

GREETING:
- Gather the class into a sitting or standing circle.
- Ask each student to come forward to say what solo song they chose, why they chose it, and how they plan to make it an exciting performance

PHYSICAL WARM-UP: Epic Story Mode
- Ask the class to take a seat facing the stage.
- Ask two volunteers to come up to the stage.
- Assign one to be Player A, the other to be Player B.
- Ask Player A to tell a story on a certain topic (i.e. Your first time camping)
- After every line, Player B will repeat what was said, but translated into "Epic Story Mode", making it as dramatic and interesting as possible.
- For example:
  - PLAYER A: *I woke up at 6am to help my dad pack the car.*
  - PLAYER B: *It's dawn, in the moments before the sun peaks above the horizon to spread its warmth, I awake with excitement and pack our transport vehicle with my wise parental figure, remembering every ration we'll need for the epic adventure that awaits us!*
- Allow other pairs to give it a try.
- Remind the students that *musical theatre is a heightened form of storytelling. As we continue to rehearse we're always trying to find the most exciting way to tell a story while remaining true to our characters.*

VOCAL WARM-UP:
- Choose 1 articulation warm-up and 2 vocal warm-ups from previous lessons (or consult **Page 58-59** in the Bonus Section)

ACTIVITY: Rehearse Ensemble Numbers
- Continue rehearsing the ensemble numbers you have chosen for the performance.
- Use formation and choreography commands from Lessons 8-9 to begin staging and blocking the numbers.
- If you have prepared scenes to precede the ensemble numbers, assign the parts and read-through them.
- Use activities from Lesson 11 to make sure the ensemble is creating an appropriate world/stage picture to support the scene and song

ACTIVITY: Review the Solo Songs
- Review the music for the solo songs for any students who may need it.
- Other students should practice on their own when not participating.

ACTIVITY: Perform Song as Monologue
- Ask a few volunteers to take the stage and perform their solo song as a monologue.
- They should take as much time with the monologue as needed, adding breaths and pauses wherever it feels natural.
- *What did you notice?*
- *Is there anything you discovered that you might be able to apply to your sung performance?*

ACTIVITY: Solo Performance Practice
- If time allows, ask a few students to come up and perform their song.
- If you have the capability, consider dimming the lights over the "audience" to create a "spotlight" feel over the stage. This can help bring focus to the performance.
- Give helpful guided feedback.

REFLECTION:
- *Drama Journal: Review the performance rubric and rate yourself based on what you feel your performance level is at this time.*

Lesson 14: Rehearsal/Dress Rehearsal

OBJECTIVE: Students will continue to work on their ensemble and solo numbers, and make preparations for their performance.

> *As a reminder, these last lesson plans can be spread across as many weeks as needed to prepare your students for the performance. Alternatively, the material for the final performance can be taught in parallel with the lessons in the beginning of this book.*

WARM-UP: Imagine your character...
- Play some calming music.
- Have the students spread out on the stage, then lie on their backs without touching anyone else
- Have them close their eyes.
- Lead them through a few quiet breathing exercises, releasing all the tension from their bodies. Start from top to bottom: Release your head, face, neck, shoulders, arms, hands, back, hip, legs, feet, toes.
- Guide them through a series of visualization techniques as the character they are portraying in their solo song:
  - *Imagine you wake up as your character*
  - *It's early in the morning, before most of the city has awoken*
  - *You eat breakfast, and get ready for your day*
  - *You take a walk down the street, focused on the one thing you really want to achieve today. What are you wearing? What's your body language like? What sounds do you hear?*
  - *You surprisingly encounter someone you dislike. What do you say to him/her? How do you react?*
  - *You see someone across the street who has fallen and needs help. How do you react?*
  - *It starts to rain, you forgot your umbrella. What do you do? A friend comes by to offer you shelter with her umbrella. What do you say to her?*
  - *etc.*
- Gather the students back into a circle and reflect on the activity.
  - *What did it feel like? Are there any details from this activity you discovered that you can incorporate into your performance?*

VOCAL WARM-UP
- Choose 1 articulation warm-up and 2 vocal warm-ups from previous lessons (or consult **Pages 58-59** in the Bonus Section)

ACTIVITY: Rehearse Ensemble Numbers
- Continue to teach and polish the ensemble numbers
- If you are using a scene, work on the transition from scene into song

ACTIVITY: Optional Rehearsal Activities
- Have the students perform the song to an empty picture frame using coaching from Lesson 10.
- Have the students perform the song without physically moving, using only facial gestures and voice variation.
- Have the students perform the song the opposite of the way your character would.

ACTIVITY: Performance Order Sign-Up
- Tell the students you're proud of the work they've done so far
- Tell them to silently walk around the playing area, making mental notes on places where they could improve their performance.
- Then tell them to create a perfect standing circle in 5 seconds. 5, 4, 3, 2....1.
- Comment on how well they worked together compared to the first time they attempted to create a perfect circle.
- Have them take a seat.
- Tell them that the order they are in right now will be the order in which they perform. (You can either take this time to write down their names in their current order, or have an assistant do it as you discuss with them the performance, or you can simply snap a picture and write down the order after class.)
- Explain to the students exactly how the performance will happen:
    - The order will be (this is just an example):
        - Solos 1-7
        - Ensemble Number #1
        - Solos 8-15
        - Ensemble Number #2
        - Solos 16-22
        - Ensemble Number #3
- Tell them there will be a one-page sheet off-stage left and right with the performance order so they can keep track of what comes next.
- Remind them that the performance is not about being perfect, but it's about showing focus and improvement and the willingness to take big risks!

REFLECTION
- Discuss with the class their general observations about their performance so far.
- *What does the class need to work on the most? Where is the class excelling?*

Lesson 15: Final Performance

OBJECTIVE: Students will present the songs they have been working on throughout the semester.

Materials:
- **Video Recorder** *(iPhone works fine, as long as it has plenty of free space! 45 minutes of 1080p HD video requires about 5.8GB of space)*
- Performance Order posted on either side of the stage

WARM-UP: Shake It Out
- Before the performance begins, lead a high-energy physical warm-up like the one below:
  - Have the players stand in a circle.
  - Explain that the students are to as a group count down from 8 while shaking out each of their limbs (In this order: Right arm, Left arm, Right leg, Left leg). Then they will count down from 7, then 6, etc. until they reach 1.
  - They should do this getting increasingly louder and louder.
  - So it will go like this:
    - ALL CLASS
      - *Right arm: "8, 7, 6, 5, 4, 3, 2, 1!"*
      - *Left arm: "8, 7, 6, 5, 4, 3, 2, 1!"*
      - *Right leg: "8, 7, 6, 5, 4, 3, 2, 1!"*
      - *Left leg: "8, 7, 6, 5, 4, 3, 2, 1!"*
      - *Right arm: "7, 6, 5, 4, 3, 2, 1!"*
      - *Left arm: "7, 6, 5, 4, 3, 2, 1!"*
      - *Right leg: "7, 6, 5, 4, 3, 2, 1!"*
      - *Left leg: "7, 6, 5, 4, 3, 2, 1!"*
      - *Right arm: "6, 5, 4, 3, 2, 1!"*
      - *…etc. until….*
      - *Right arm: "1!"*
      - *Left arm: "1!"*
      - *Right leg: "1!"*
      - *Left leg: "1!"*
  - For a super quick version of the game, have the students count down by even numbers until they get to 1: 8…, 6…., 4…, 2…, 1!

VOCAL WARM-UP
- Choose 1 articulation warm-up and 2 vocal warm-ups from previous lessons (or consult **Page 58-59** in the Bonus Section)

PERFORMANCE

- Welcome the audience and give a brief overview of what the class has been working on all semester
- Go through the line-up as listed on the Performance Sheet.
- Jump in and assist as need to help the performance run smoothly.
- Make sure everyone participates in the applause after each number.
- Here are some tips for executing a successful sharing day:
  - **Be organized, clear and concise.** Parents don't want to see a fumbling teacher, and kids will get antsy if they don't have specific direction. Make sure you (and your accompanist) have your own list of the Performance Order and confidently guide the students from number to number. When introducing the performance, be concise. Cover how excited you are to share what you and the kids have been working on, the goals that the class have been working toward, what they're about to see, and a short personal tidbit about the program.
  - **Keep it positive.** Don't ever apologize for things not being as polished as they could be because of lack of time or resources. Instead mention how impressed you are with what the kids accomplished in such little time. If you know a particular song is going to be a little rough, introduce it just as you would any other. Then jump in and give the kids support as they need it.
  - **Have clean transitions.** The moments after a big ensemble number are the most crucial moments to maintain control of the environment. Simply telling the students as their laughing and talking "please go back to your seats" will not be effective. Instead, instantly regain their focus through a simple breathing exercise you've been practicing all semester. *Everyone take a breath in, breath out, silently head back to your seats in 3 counts. 3...2.....1. I'd now like to introduce...*
  - **Wait for applause.** Remind the students to freeze for 3 seconds after every number to soak in the applause.
  - **Finish with a bang.** End the presentation with a song that you know will have everyone leaving with a giant smile on their face. Even though you may be in an informal environment, choreograph a clean simple bow by the ensemble at the end. This is good practice for the students and a will make the performance feel more professional for the parents. After the bows ask the class to create *1 Clump* with *3 Levels* facing the audience - this will be the opportunity for the parents to take a group picture.

REFLECTION

- Thank the students for all the hard work and talent in putting on a wonderful show.
- Thank the parents for allowing their children to participate.

Lesson 16: Reflection & Assessment

OBJECTIVE: Students will reflect on what they've learned through a discussion and watching the video of their performance.

MATERIALS:
- Performance Rubric for each student
- Video of the final performance

WARM-UP: Group Massage
- Gather the class into a sitting circle.
- Ask the class to turn to their left and gently start massaging the shoulders of the student in front of them.
- After awhile, have them switch the other way.
- As this is happening, tell the students this massage is a reward for a job well done. Talk about all the positive things you noticed about the performance, and how proud you are of how far they have come.
- Go around the circle with each student describing their experience this semester in one word.
- Take out a soft ball. Tell the class you're going to ask a question, then pass this ball to someone. Whoever receives the ball must answer, then pass to another student.
- Sample questions:
  - *How did you view musical theatre before this class?*
  - *How do you view musical theatre now?*
  - *Do you feel you have a better understanding of how to effectively tell stories on stage?*
  - *If you were cast in a musical, do you feel you would be prepared?*

ACTIVITY: Video Recording Assessment
- Pass out a blank Performance Rubric (see **Page 47**)
- Tell them to fill in their own name in one of the columns, and the name of the ensemble numbers in the other columns.
- Tell the class they are going to watch the video of their performance
- They are to grade their own performance, plus all the ensemble performances by filling out the rubric.
- You can take a break half-way through to play a fun drama game (like Zip, Zap, Zop or Bippity Bippity Bop) if the students start to get antsy

REFLECTION:
- Have the class answer the following questions in their drama journals:
  - *This is what I did well:*
  - *This is what I think I need to improve:*
  - *This is my recommendation for a plan for improvement:*
  - *This is my favorite thing I discovered about myself:*
  - *Other observations:*
- *Drama Journal: In your journal, write a short letter to someone who is interested in acting but has never acted before. Share a bit of your experience.*

Bonus Material

A.	Tongue Twisters

B.	Vocal Warm-Ups

C.	"My Treehouse" Lyric Sheet

D.	"My Treehouse" Piano-Vocal Sheet Music

E.	Newsies Article Excerpt

A. Tongue Twisters

- Unique New York
- Three free throws
- Red Leather, Yellow Leather
- I thought a thought
  But the thought I thought wasn't the
  thought I thought I thought
- One-One was a racehorse
  Two-Two was one, too
  When One-One won one race
  Two-Two won one, too
- Say this sharply, say this sweetly
  Say this shortly, say this softly
  Say this sixteen times very quickly
- Rubber Baby Buggy Bumpers!
- Silly Sally swiftly shooed seven silly sheep
  The seven silly sheep Silly Sally shooed
  Shilly-shallied south
- These sheep shouldn't sleep in a shack
  Sheep should sleep in a shed.
- Red Bulb Blue Bulb Red Bulb Blue Bulb
- Red Blood Blue Blood
- I wish to wish the wish you wish to wish, but if you
  wish the wish the witch wishes, I won't wish the
  wish you wish to wish
- She sells seashells on the seashore
- Mix a box of mixed biscuits with a boxed biscuit
  mixer
- A proper copper coffee pot
- Toy boat. Toy boat. Toy boat.
- Betty bought butter but the butter was bitter, so
  Betty bought better butter to make the bitter
  butter better

- If the thought I thought I thought had been the
  thought I thought, I wouldn't have thought so
  much
- How much wood could a wood chuck; chuck if a
  wood chuck could chuck wood
- Comical economists
- Which wristwatches are Swiss wristwatches?
- Peter Piper picked a peck of pickled peppers
  A peck of pickled peppers Peter Piper picked
  If Peter Piper picked a peck of pickled peppers
  Where's the peck of pickled peppers Peter Piper
  picked?
- Sasha sews slightly slashed sheets shut
- She should shun the shinning sun
- The big black back brake broke badly
- The big beautiful blue balloon burst
- A shapeless sash sags slowly
- Smelly shoes and socks shock sisters
- Dick kicks sticky bricks
- Shave a single shingle thin
- Stick strictly six sticks stumps
- Cinnamon aluminum linoleum
- New York is unanimously universally unique
- Cooks cook cupcakes quickly
- Flora's freshly fried fish
- A bragging baker baked black bread
- Buy blue blueberry biscuits before bedtime
- She sold six shabby sheared sheep on ship
- The sixth sick sheik's son slept
- These thousand tricky tongue twisters trip
  thrillingly off the tongue

B. Vocal Warm-Ups

Ha ha ha ha ha ha ha.   Ha ha ha ha ha ha ha.

Keep repeating a half-step higher, 4 or 5 more times.

Me_____ May_____ Mo Oh oh.   Me_____ May_____ Mo Oh oh.

Keep repeating a half-step higher, 6 or 7 more times.

Ma-ma made me mash my M & M's. Oh my!   Ma-ma made me mash my M & M's. Oh my!

Keep repeating a half-step lower, 6 or 7 more times.

Sup-er dup-er dou-ble bub-ble gum.   Sup-er dup-er dou-ble bub-ble gum.

Keep repeating a half-step higher, 6 or 7 more times.

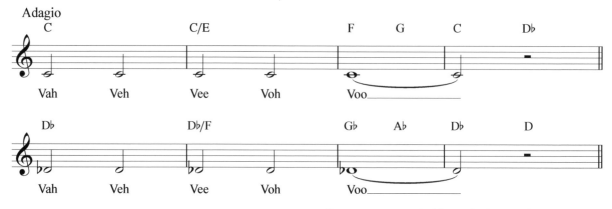

Vah   Veh   Vee   Voh   Voo_____

Vah   Veh   Vee   Voh   Voo_____

Keep repeating a half-step higher, 6 or 7 more times.

58

C   Db

Po po ka ta pe-tal Po po ka ta pe-tal Po po ka ta pe-tal Po po ka ta pe-tal Po.

Keep repeating a half-step higher, 5 or 6 more times.

Bum - ble - bee___ Bum - ble - bee___ Bum - ble - bee___ Bum - ble - bee.

Bum - ble - bee___ Bum - ble - bee___ Bum - ble - bee___ Bum - ble - bee.

Keep repeating a half-step higher, 4 or 5 more times.

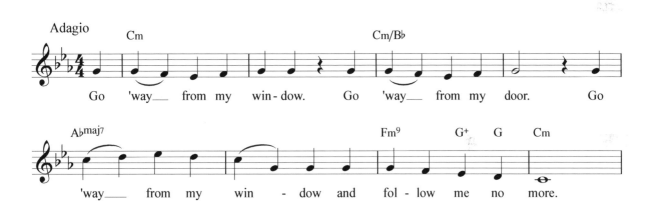

Go 'way___ from my win-dow. Go 'way___ from my door. Go

'way___ from my win - dow and fol - low me no more.

Every so often ask the students to sing in a fun style:
- *Like an opera singer*
- *Like a rock star*
- *Like an evil witch*
- *Like a robot*
- *Like a king*
- *Like a really shy child*
- *Like a lion*
- *Like a tiny bird*
- *What do YOU think we should sing like?* Ask for suggestions.

C. "My Treehouse" Lyric Sheet

From *The Most Epic Birthday Party Ever*

Music and Lyrics by
Denver Casado and Betina Hershey Russo

SKYLER

When I was 8 and was afraid to go to my first piano recital, I hid in this treehouse. I felt safe.
When I was 10 and my dad yelled at me for lying, this is where I ran to. I felt protected. And
now that I'm 12, and everyone has left me on my birthday...well, what better place to be?

JUST ME UP HERE IN MY TREE HOUSE
NOT MUCH TO FEAR IN MY TREE HOUSE
I'M ALL ALONE
BUT I FEEL LIKE I BELONG HERE

JUST ME AND LEAVES IN MY TREE HOUSE
A CALMING BREEZE IN MY TREE HOUSE
IT MAY SOUND SIMPLE
BUT I CANT DO MUCH WRONG HERE

'CAUSE IN MY TREE
FREEDOM REIGNS
SO MUCH TO SEE
ABOVE THE PLAINS
JUST LITTLE ME
NO ONE COMPLAINS

SO SAFE AND SOUND IN MY TREE HOUSE
I WON'T BE FOUND IN MY TREE HOUSE
UNLESS I WANT TO BE

D. "My Treehouse" Piano-Vocal Sheet Music

SKYLER:
When I was 8 and was afraid to go to my first piano recital, I hid in this treehouse. I felt safe.
When I was 10 and my dad yelled at me for lying, this is where I ran to. I felt protected.
And now that I'm 12, and everyone has left me on my birthday...well, what better place to be?

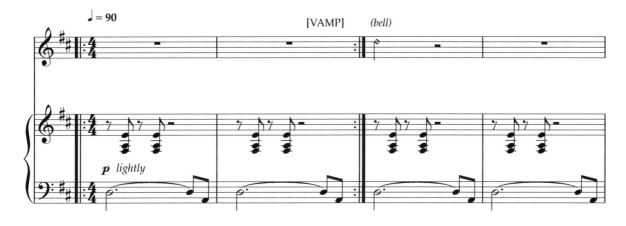

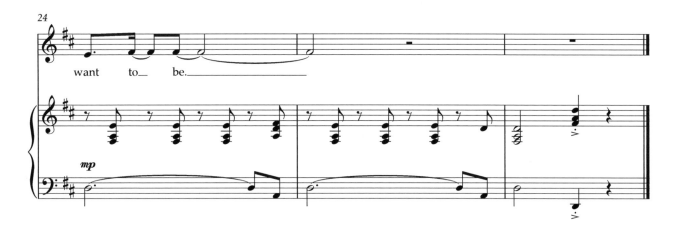

want   to__   be._____

E. Newsies Article Excerpt

New York City "Newsies" Strike Against the World and Journal, 1899

The July, 1899 strike of New York City newspaper delivery boys, was a response to a decision by *The Evening World* and *The Evening Journal*, parts of the national Pulitzer and Hearst newspaper empires, to raise the wholesale price they charged street vendors. The "Newsies" organized and demanded that the original price be restored. When Pulitzer and Hearst refused, 300 boys went on strike. One boy was quoted as saying, "We're here fer our rights an' we will die defendin"em." Eventually the strike spread throughout all New York City; then to New Jersey, Connecticut, Massachusetts & Rhone Island. The strike lasted from July 18, 1899 through August 2, 1899. The publishers ultimately decided to offer the "Newsies" a compromise, which they accepted. The new higher price for the newspapers remained, but the companies agreed to buy back all unsold papers at a 100% refund. During their short strike, the "Newsies" demonstrated that workers, even children, could fight for rights against powerful employers and be successful.

Sources: www.fortunecity.com/meltingpot/offord/192/articles; *The New York Times, What We Saw, 1851-2001* by Kelly Delia, Jason Sarofsky, Christine Roblin and Jaimee Kahn

Acknowledgements

A special thank you to all of the teaching artists I've worked with who introduced me to many ideas found in this handbook, including: Betina Hershey, Sophia Chapadjiev, Robby Stamper and Debra Sue Lorenzen.

About Beat by Beat Press

Beat by Beat Press is the world's fastest growing publisher of original, high-quality musicals for kids, songs for kids and teaching drama resources. The materials are created by a team of professional playwrights and arts educators in New York City and Los Angeles. Since launching in 2011, Beat by Beat shows have premiered in over 60 countries and its website receives over 75,000 visitors a month.

Other Books from Beat by Beat

www.bbbpress.com

Printed in Great Britain
by Amazon